Andrea Palladio Vicenza
guide

text by
Guido Beltramini

photography by
Pino Guidolotti

Marsilio

Front cover
© Photo Pino Guidolotti

The map on pages 4-5 is drawn
by Petralito Rotiroti Associati

Graphic design
Tapiro, Venezia

© 2008 by Marsilio Editori® s.p.a.
in Venezia

ISBN 88-317-9686

www.marsilioeditori.it

Contents

Palladio in Vicenza

1.
Villa Trissino at Cricoli

Although this villa cannot be attributed to Palladio with any certainty, it is an emblematic building marking the beginning of a legend. According to tradition, in the second half of the 1530s, it was here that the Vicentine noble Giangiorgio Trissino (1478-1550) met the young stonemason Andrea di Pietro who was involved in the construction of the villa. Immediately realizing the young man's great potential and talent, Trissino took charge of his education and introduced him to the aristocratic circles in Vicenza. As a result, the young stonemason was soon transformed into the architect with the classical-sounding name of 'Palladio'.

Giangiorgio Trissino was a man of letters and wrote works of theater and grammar. In Rome he had been welcomed into the close cultural circle of Pope Leo x (Giovanni de' Medici), where he had met Raphael. A keen connoisseur of architecture (his drawings for his own urban palace and the draft of a treatise on architecture survive), Trissino was probably personally responsible for remodeling the family villa he had inherited from his father at Cricoli, just outside Vicenza.

Trissino did not demolish the pre-existing building, but redesigned it around the principal façade facing south, a kind of manifesto testifying to his devotion to the new architectural culture based on the rediscovery of ancient Rome. Between the two existing towers, Trissino inserted a loggia with two orders of arches, directly inspired by Raphael's façade for the Villa Madama in Rome as published by Sebastiano Serlio in the *Terzo Libro dell'Architettura* (Venice 1540). Trissino reorganized the spaces into a sequence of side rooms, differing in dimensions but linked by a system of ratios (1:1; 2:3; and 1:2). This schema would later become a key element in Palladio's own design method. Work on the building was completed by 1538. In the late eighteenth century, the Vicentine architect Ottone Calderari radically altered the structure and further work in the early twentieth century canceled out the last traces of the Gothic building in a latter-day 'Palladization'.

2.
Church of Santa Maria dei Servi. Portal

The portal of Santa Maria dei Servi bears the inscribed date 1531. The commission for its construction, worth two hundred ducats, was given to Gerolamo Pittoni and Giacomo da Porlezza by Francesco Godi. Gerolamo and Giacomo were the renowned 'Pedemuro Masters' (after the village where they had a workshop) and among their assistants, from 1524, was the young stonemason Andrea di Pietro, yet to become Palladio.

Compared to the rest of the Pedemuro Masters' known work, the portal of Santa Maria dei Servi stands out for the design quality of its architectural elements which are very close to Venetian buildings by Jacopo Sansovino. The portal may thus be an early design by the young Andrea, who over the years gradually specialized as the supervisor of architectural projects in the workshop.

3.
Palazzo Civena

The first urban palace Palladio built in Vicenza was constructed for the Civena brothers (Giovanni Giacomo, Pier Antonio, Vincenzo, and Francesco). The date '1540' engraved on the foundation medal (now in the Museo Civico, Vicenza) indicates the year when the foundation stone was laid. The building was probably finished twenty-four months later, six months before work began on the much larger Palazzo Thiene. Palazzo Civena has had a troubled history: clumsily altered by Domenico Cerato in 1750, it was half destroyed by bombing during World War II and then reconstructed, only for its façade to be subjected to a recent unbecoming repainting.

Palazzo Civena was not included in the *Quattro Libri*, but several autograph drawings by Palladio document the various solutions he elaborated at the design stage. Today's distribution of internal spaces does not follow Palladio's definitive idea but is the outcome of Cerato's heavy-handed work, lengthening the atrium and modifying the stairs. The original plan, however, may be reconstructed thanks to a drawing published in 1776 by Ottavio Bertotti Scamozzi (who claimed to have obtained it from the owners): the grouping of rooms in two nuclei set on either side of the atrium with a *serliana* providing the filter to the exterior does in fact appear to be close to Palladio's villa projects in the same years. The very early date of the project means Palazzo Civena is valuable evidence of Palladio's youthful activity and his architectural ideas before the decisive journey to Rome in 1541. As with the villa at Cricoli, this building marked a break with contemporary building practice in Vicenza: the traditional polyforate window at the center of the façade has been replaced with a regular sequence of bays rhythmically ordered by paired pilasters. In this respect, Palladio was evidently inspired by early sixteenth-century palaces in Rome but clearly not from first-hand knowledge of them: the building's façade is devoid of any real plastic force and almost looks like a paper cut-out. Moreover, the architectural vocabulary is worked through models from the Veneto rather than Roman ones, and especially Giovanni Maria Falconetto's buildings in Padua.

The palace as it appears today was created by joining two buildings once separated by an alley called the Stradella Due Ruote (one of the buildings probably dates from 1566), following a request made by Vincenzo Pojana to the Vicenza City Council in 1561. The attribution to Palladio is based neither on documentary evidence nor on autograph drawings, but rather on the architectural quality of the organization of the *piano nobile* with its order embracing two whole floors, as well as the design of various details such as the elegant fleshy Composite capitals and the trabeation. Elements such as the pilasters with no entasis (i.e. the characteristic swelling up to a third of the shaft's height), however, are so out of keeping with Palladio's vocabulary of the 1560s as to suggest that the design of the left-hand part of the palace was the result of a youthful project only later extended to include the neighboring building in the 1560s, when Pojana decided to enlarge his residence. This would also explain the differences in the form of the basement in the two halves of the building.

4.
Palazzo Pojana

5.
Palazzo Thiene

In October 1542, Marcantonio and Adriano Thiene began a grandiose project to remodel their fifteenth-century family palace, which would have occupied an entire street block of 54 x 62 meters and faced onto Vicenza's main thoroughfare (now Corso Palladio). The rich powerful and sophisticated Thiene brothers belonged to the great Italian nobility that moved with ease between the major European courts. They therefore required a domestic setting reflecting their cosmopolitan taste and suitable for noble guests. At the same time, as members of a political faction in the city's aristocracy, they wanted to build a princely palace emphasizing their role in the city and as a sign of their seignorial power.

When the English architect Inigo Jones visited the palace in 1614, he noted information directly garnered from Vincenzo Scamozzi and Palma il Giovane: "these designs were made by Giulio Romano and executed by Palladio". The original conception of the Palazzo Thiene should thus probably be attributed to the mature and expert Giulio Romano (from 1573 he was at the Mantua court of the Gonzaga with whom the Thiene were in close contact), while the young Palladio was responsible for the executive project and construction of the building. His role obviously became much more important after Giulio's death in 1546.

There are a number of clearly recognizable elements attributable to Giulio Romano and alien to Palladio's vocabulary: the four-column atrium is almost identical to that of the Palazzo del Te (even though Palladio modified the vaulting system); the windows and the ground-story façades onto the street and courtyard are also by Giulio, while Palladio was responsible for the trabeation and capitals on the *piano nobile*.

Work began on the building in 1542. In December of the same year, Giulio Romano visited Vicenza for two weeks to advise on the Basilica loggias. He probably supplied the preliminary design for the Palazzo Thiene on this occasion. Work progressed slowly: the date 1556 is inscribed on the external façade, while in the courtyard we find the date 1558. Adriano Thiene died in France in 1552 and when Marcantonio's son Giulio became Marchese di Scandiano, the family interests gradually shifted to Ferrara. As a result, only a small part of the grandiose project was ever realized. In any case, probably neither the Venetians nor the other Vicentine nobles would have been willing to accept the presence of such a regal private residence in the city center.

6.
Palazzo Iseppo Porto

Iseppo (Giuseppe) Porto very probably wished to build a great palace in the Contrada dei Porti to vie with the building his brothers-in-law, Adriano and Marcantonio Thiene, had begun only a stone's throw away, in 1542. Iseppo's marriage to Livia Thiene in the first half of the 1540s may explain in part how the commission went to Andrea Palladio.

Allied with the Thiene, the Porto were one of the richest and most powerful families in the city. The palaces of the family's various branches stood along the Contrada that still bears their name today. Iseppo was an influential figure responsible for various matters in the public administration of the city. On several occasions his activities were associated with public appointments entrusted to Palladio. The two were clearly on much friendlier terms than a normal patron-architect relationship. Indeed, thirty years after the project for Iseppo's urban palace, Palladio designed and began to build a great villa for him at Molina di Malo, though it was never completed. The two friends died in the same year, 1580.

The palace was already habitable by December 1549, though less than half the façade was standing and would only be completed three years later, in 1552. Numerous autograph drawings by Palladio record the complex design process. From the outset, he planned two distinct residential blocks, one to stand along the street and the other contiguous to the rear wall of the courtyard. In the *Quattro Libri,* a majestic courtyard with giant Composite columns connects the two blocks: this is clearly a re-elaboration of the original idea for the purposes of publication.

Compared with the Palazzo Civena, built only a few years earlier, the Palazzo Porto fully illustrates the extent of Palladio's development after his stay in Rome in 1541 and his knowledge of both antique and contemporary architecture. Bramante's model of Palazzo Caprini is reinterpreted, but Palladio took into account the Vicentine custom of living on the ground floor which is raised as a result. The splendid four-columned atrium is Palladio's reinterpretation of Vitruvian spaces with some influences from traditional Vicentine types. Paolo Veronese and Domenico Brusasorzi frescoed the two rooms to the left of the atrium, while the stuccoes are by Ridolfi. At attic level, the statues of Iseppo and his son Leonida dressed in ancient Roman garb watch over the visitors' entrance to their house.

7.
Palazzo della Ragione.
Loggias

From 1481 to 1494, Tommaso Formenton girded a two-story loggia round the Palazzo della Ragione, seat of the Magistrature of Vicenza, the lower order being used to accommodate a row of shops. Two years after work had been completed the south-west corner collapsed and for over forty years the Vicentines failed to agree how it should be reconstructed. As the decades passed, the most celebrated architects working in the region were summoned to address the problem: Antonio Rizzo and Giorgio Spavento (1496), Antonio Scarpagnino (1525), Jacopo Sansovino (1538), Sebastiano Serlio (1539), Michele Sanmicheli (1541) and, lastly, Giulio Romano (1542) who made the unusual proposal of raising the level of Piazza delle Erbe and isolating the building at the center of a large square.

Despite such illustrious advice, in March 1546 the City Council approved a project by Andrea Palladio, a relatively unknown local architect, who was barely thirty-eight years old at the time but the protégé of Giangiorgio Trissino. The appointment of Palladio was undoubtedly a great victory for Trissino, who was able to marshal considerable consensus for this choice. As a precaution, the young architect was to be flanked by the expert and reliable Giovanni da Pedemuro. Moreover, to dispel all doubts, the Council requested that a wooden model of one of the proposed arches be constructed and put on public view. In May 1549, after another three years of discussions which had even seen the projects by Rizzo-Spavento and Giulio Romano reappraised, Andrea Palladio's scheme received definitive approval thanks also to the forceful public backing of Gerolamo Chiericati and Alvise Valmarana, who were to turn to Palladio for their own family palaces in later years. Various autograph drawings survive documenting the gradual honing of the project concept, from a primitive version of 1546 to the designs for the structure eventually built.

The solution that Palladio proposed was, so to speak, a 'flexible' structure since it had to take into account the alignments with the openings and passageways of the pre-existing fifteenth-century palace. The system is based on

the repetition of the *serliana* (i.e. an open arch of constant width) flanked by two narrower rectangular side openings of variable breadth to adjust to the different bay widths. This expedient is most evident in the corner arches where the rectangular openings with architraves are extremely narrow, but is actually present in all the bays since their width always varies slightly. The *serliana* (which Sebastiano Serlio published in *Book IV* of his treatise, Venice 1537) is actually a translation into classical language of the Gothic *polifora* used for the first time by Donato Bramante at Santa Maria del Popolo in Rome and previously adopted in the Veneto by Jacopo Sansovino for the Libreria Marciana in 1537. The direct source for Palladio's idea in Vicenza, however, may be found in the interior of the monastery church of San Benedetto in Polirone, remodeled starting in 1540 by Giulio Romano, who also exploited *serliane* to accommodate the variations in width of the fourteenth-century bays of the old church. With a certain rhetorical flourish, Palladio himself adopted the term 'basilica' to describe the Palazzo della Ragione, girded by its new stone loggias as homage to the ancient Roman basilica used for political debate and trading. The work on the loggias marked a turning point in Palladio's career. Now he had become the official architect of the city of Vicenza, responsible for a grandiose work entirely made of stone (which at the final reckoning would cost the notable sum of 60,000 ducats) without equal in sixteenth-century Venetian architecture. He would have to wait until the 1560s before another commission of such importance came his way with the church of San Giorgio in Venice. At the same time, the salary of 5 ducats per month was an indispensable life-long source of income for Palladio and his family. Building work proceeded slowly: the ground floor ranges of western and northern arcades were finished in 1561, the second story was begun in 1564 and completed in 1597 (seventeen years after Palladio's death), while the façade giving onto Piazza delle Erbe was only finally completed in 1614.

8.
Palazzo Chiericati

In November 1550 Girolamo Chiericati registered a payment to Palladio in his account books for the designs of a city palace, drawn up at the beginning of the year. In the same month Girolamo was appointed to supervise the work on the loggias of the Basilica, which had begun in May 1549. This was no coincidence. Like Trissino, Chiericati was among those who advocated entrusting this prestigious public commission to the young architect. Indeed he had personally canvassed on the architect's behalf in the City Council and he would turn to him for the design of his own house. Moreover, a few years later, his brother Giovanni would commission Palladio to design a villa at Vancimuglio.

In 1546 Girolamo had inherited a few old houses looking onto the so-called Piazza dell'Isola, an open space on the southern outskirts of the city. The name (*isola* means 'island') was due to the fact that the plot was bounded on two side by rivers—the Retrone and the Bacchiglione—just before their confluence. As the city's river port, the Isola was where the timber and cattle markets were held. The small size of the old existing houses induced Girolamo to ask the City Council for permission to utilize a strip of roughly four and a half meters of public land in front of his property for the portico of his new house, while allowing its public use. Once the request was accepted, building work began immediately in 1551 but then came to a halt in 1557 upon the death of Girolamo. His son Valerio only finished the internal decoration, employing an extraordinary team of artists, including Ridolfi, Zelotti, Fasolo, Forbicini, and Battista Franco.

For more than a century, Palazzo Chiericati remained a majestic fragment (similar to the present state of the Palazzo Porto in Piazza Castello), interrupted half way along its fourth bay as documented in the *Pianta Angelica* and various travelers' sketchbooks. Only at the end of the seventeenth century would the *palazzo* be completed according to the design in the *Quattro Libri*. Several autograph drawings by Palladio survive to document the evolution of the project, from the

initial solution in which the portico only juts out at the center of the façade (as well as being surmounted by a pediment, like the one later made for the Villa Cornaro), to the solution eventually adopted. The plan was determined by the site's narrow dimensions: a central two-apsed atrium is flanked by two nuclei of three rooms with harmoniously linked dimensions (3:2; 1:1; 3:5), each with its own spiral service stair and monumental flight of steps to one side of the back loggia (another element also found in the Villa Pisani and the Villa Cornaro). To give the palace a grand aspect but also to protect it from the frequent floods (and the cattle sold in front on market days), Palladio raised the building on a podium whose central section has a flight of steps clearly adapted from an antique temple.

The extraordinary novelty of the Palazzo Chiericati in the world of Renaissance urban residences owes a great deal to Palladio's ingenious interpretation of the site: a great open space on the margins of the city in front of the river. Moreover, the context led to the building having an ambiguous character as both *palazzo* and *villa suburbana*. Not surprisingly there are many affinities with the Villa Cornaro at Piombino and the Villa Pisani at Montagnana built at about the same time. On the Piazza dell'Isola, Palladio set a façade with a two-story loggia capable of visually framing the open space-almost like the front of an imaginary ancient Roman forum. Even though superimposed loggias are to be found in Peruzzi's Palazzo Massimo in Rome and in the antique courtyard of Moroni's Palazzo Bo in Padua, Palladio's use of loggias in the façade of the Palazzo Chiericati is absolutely new in terms of its power and self-conscious expression. The Basilica and Palazzo Chiericati testify to Palladio's definitive passage from the eclecticism of his early years to the full maturity of a language in which the stimuli and sources of both antique and contemporary architecture had been absorbed into his own characteristic system. This is the first time the side of a loggia is closed by a wall section containing an arch. Borrowed from the Portico di Ottavia in Rome, this solution was to become the usual practice in the temple fronts of Palladio's villas.

Begun in 1482 to a design by Lorenzo da Bologna, the apse of Vicenza cathedral was still unfinished in 1531. Temporary roofing was erected in 1540 when Vicenza had been designated for the Church Council eventually held, however, in Trent. Only in 1557 did the Vicenza City Council finally receive the necessary financial means from the Republic of Venice—thanks to a bequest from Bishop Zeno at the beginning of the century—and could therefore set about completing the work.

In charge of the project, Palladio very probably drafted an overall design which was executed, however, in two stages: from 1558 to 1559, the main cornice was built over the windows and the drum raised, while from 1564 to January 1566, the dome was constructed. The characteristic form of the lantern, abstract with no decoration, is also found on the top of the cupolas of San Giorgio Maggiore in Venice (designed around the same time) and in some of Palladio's reconstructions of centrally planned antique temples, such as the Mausoleum of Romulus on the Via Appia.

In 1560 Paolo Almerico asked the cathedral Chapter for permission to erect a portal at his own expense on the north side of the cathedral as an entrance to the chapel of San Giovanni Evangelista. This is the same Paolo Almerico who, a few years later, would entrust Palladio with the commission to build the Villa Rotonda. The portal was opened in 1565, probably on the occasion of the solemn entrance of Bishop Matteo Priuli. In the absence of documents or autograph drawings, the attribution to Palladio is based on both the portal's affinities with antique models well known to the architect (such as the portal of the Temple of Fortuna Virile) and the design of the lateral portals of the church of San Pietro di Castello in Venice, which he designed in 1558.

9.
Vicenza Cathedral. Dome and Side Portal

In 1560 Palladio designed the façade of Bernardo Schio's house in Vicenza, in the neighborhood of the Ponte Pusterla. Preoccupied at the time with a series of Venetian projects requiring his almost permanent presence in the capital, Palladio neglected supervising the work on the Palazzo Schio to such an extent that the master mason in charge of building had to interrupt work for want of clear instructions. Following Bernardo's death, his widow showed no interest in continuing the work which was only eventually completed by Bernardo's brother Fabrizio in 1574-1575 after stones and other construction materials had lain piled up in the courtyard for many years.

10.
Palazzo Schio. Façade

Although known as 'Palladio's House', this building has no connection with the residence of the Vicentine architect. Its smallish size compared to the monumental scale of other Palladian palaces led to it being mistakenly named by those who had eagerly sought some visible sign of the architect's home in the city. The Venetian Great Council had actually demanded that the notary Pietro Cogollo remodel the façade of his fifteenth-century house as a contribution to the city's 'decorum', making it a condition for his application for Vicentine citizenship. Moreover, the financial investment in the work had to be no less than 250 ducats.

In the absence of documents and autograph designs, there is still no general agreement on the attribution of this elegant façade to Palladio. But, given the very clever architectural solution and the great care over details, it is difficult to see who else could have been responsible. The restrictions of a narrow lot and the impossibility of opening windows at the center of the *piano nobile* (because of an existing fireplace and flue) led Palladio to emphasize the façade's central axis. He did so by building a structure with a ground-floor arch flanked by half-columns, while on the upper story he created a kind of tabernacle framing a fresco by Giovanni Antonio Fasolo.

The ground-floor arch is flanked by two rectangular spaces illuminating and providing access to the portico and creating a kind of *serliana*, along the lines of that in the Basilica. The overall result is a composition with a surprising monumental and expressive force given the simplicity of the means available.

11.
Casa Cogollo, or 'Palladio's House'

Engraved on the foundation medal of this building are the date 1566 and a profile of Isabella Nogarola Valmarana. Although she signed the construction contracts with the builders in December 1565, it was her deceased husband, Giovanni Alvise (d. 1558), who had played the key role in choosing Palladio as the architect for the family palace. In 1549, along with Girolamo Chiericati and Trissino, Giovanni Alvise Valmarana had publicly supported Palladio's project for the loggias of the Basilica. This was evidently on the basis of an opinion formed six years earlier when Giovanni Alvise had supervised the execution of temporary structures, conceived by Palladio under Trissino's direction, to honor the entrance into Vicenza of Bishop Ridolfi (1543). Palladio was also to design the Valmarana chapel in the church of Santa Corona, which would eventually hold the mortal remains of Giovanni Alvise and Isabella after receiving the commission from their son Leonardo.

The Valmarana family had owned buildings on the site for the new sixteenth-century palace from the end of the fifteenth century. Over the years, prior to Palladio's renovation, they had gradually been joined together. The irregular plan of the rooms is doubtless due to the oblique orientation of the façade and the pre-existing walls. In this sense, the Olympian regularity of the palace illustrated in the *Quattro Libri* was clearly the product of Palladio's usual idealization. Indeed, not only was the extension to the palace beyond the square courtyard never built, but it seems never to have been seriously contemplated by Leonardo Valmarana who bought up neighboring properties rather than continue with the construction of the family palace.

The façade of the Palazzo Valmarana is one of Palladio's most extraordinary and most original works. For the first time in a palace, a giant order stretches up for the entire height of the building. This solution was obviously the outcome of Palladio's experiments with the fronts of religious buildings such as the almost contemporary façade of the church of San Francesco della Vigna. Just as the nave and aisles are projected onto the same plane in the Venetian church, so too in the façade of the Palazzo Valmarana there is a clear stratification of two systems: the giant Composite order of six pilasters seems to be superimposed on the smaller order of Corinthian pilasters. This is far more evident at the edges where the absence of the final pilaster reveals the lower order supporting a bas-relief of a soldier with the Valmarana coat of arms.

The compositional logic of these civil and religious façades derives from Palladio's draftsmanship rather than from any abstract geometrical elaborations. This is particularly true of the orthogonal projections in which he visualizes projects and reconstructs ancient buildings, enabling him to control the relationships between the building's interior and exterior very closely. In this specific case the giant pilasters raised on plinths are very reminiscent of the free-standing columns on pedestals in the temple of Minerva at Assisi.

13.
Villa Almerico Capra, or 'La Rotonda'

Although the Villa Rotonda is the universal icon of the Palladian 'villa', in reality its owner considered it an urban residence or, rather, a 'suburban' house. Paolo Almerico sold his palace in the city in order to move to this villa just beyond the city walls and Palladio published it among his palaces, and not among the villas, in the *Quattro Libri*. Moreover, the villa stands alone on top of a small hill and originally there were no annexed farm buildings.

Canon Paolo Almerico, for whom Palladio designed the villa in 1566, was a man of changing fortunes. He had returned to Vicenza after a brilliant career at the Papal court. By 1569 he was already living in the villa although still incomplete. Then, in 1591, two years after Almerico's death, the villa was sold to the brothers Odorico and Marco Capra who completed the building work. Having taken over from Palladio as architect after 1580, Scamozzi basically completed the project with some alterations which recent studies tend to consider very unimaginative. The building is sumptuously adorned with works by Lorenzo Rubini and Giambattista Albanese (statues), Agostino Rubini, Ottavio Ridolfi, Bascapè, Domenico Fontana and possibly Alessandro Vittoria (the plastic decorations of the ceilings and fireplaces), Anselmo Canera, Bernardino India, Alessandro Maganza and, much later, Ludovico Dorigny (pictorial decorations).

Certainly not a 'villa-farm', the Villa Rotonda is rather a villa-temple, an abstraction, mirroring a higher order and harmony. With its corners oriented to the four compass points, it is primarily meant to be read in terms of its volumes—a cube and a sphere—almost alluding to the primary solids in Plato's universe. There were certainly several sources for such a centrally planned residential building: from the projects by Francesco di Giorgio based on Hadrian's Villa, or the study of Varro, to Mantegna's house in Mantua (or his Camera degli Sposi in the Palazzo Ducale), and Raphael's project for the Villa Madama. The fact remains that the Villa Rotonda is unique in the architecture of all time. By building a self-contained villa, perfectly corresponding to itself, Palladio almost seems to have been bent on constructing an ideal model of his own architecture.

Built from 1570 to 1575 for the Vicentine noble Montano Barbarano, this sumptuous residence is the only great urban palace that Palladio succeeded in building in its entirety. At least three different autograph projects survive (preserved in London) documenting alternative ideas for the plan. They are all quite different from the executed project suggesting a very complex design process. Barbarano, in fact, had asked Palladio to include various houses already belonging to the family in the area of the new palace. Moreover, after work had begun, Barbarano acquired another house adjoining the property and this explains the asymmetrical positioning of the entrance portal. In any case, the restrictions due to the site and a demanding patron provided a challenge calling for bold and subtle solutions. Palladio's masterly work is the outcome of a sophisticated 'redevelopment' scheme blending the diverse pre-existing structures into a unified whole.

On the ground floor, a magnificent four-columned atrium welds together the two pre-existing building lots. For this purpose Palladio had to solve two problems: the static problem of how to support the floor of the great hall on the *piano nobile* and the compositional problem of how to restore a symmetrical appearance to the interiors conditioned by the oblique course of the perimeter walls from the pre-existing houses.

Taking as a model the basilica of the Theater of Marcellus in Rome, Palladio divided the interior into three aisles, placing four Ionic columns centrally, thus reducing the span of the central cross-vaults, braced by lateral barrel vaults. He thus created a very efficient system, perfectly suited to bearing the floor of the hall. The central columns were then tied to the perimeter walls by fragments of rectilinear trabeation to absorb the irregularities of the atrium plan. He thus introduced a kind of system of *serliane*, an expedient conceptually similar to that in the loggias of the Basilica. Palladio even adopted an unusual type of Ionic capital—derived from the Temple of Saturn in the Roman Forum—allowing him to mask the slight but significant rotations necessary to align the columns and half columns.

For the palace decoration, Montano turned to some of the greatest artists of the day: Battista Zelotti, who had already worked on the interiors of Palladio's Villa Emo at Fanzolo, Anselmo Canera, and Andrea Vicentino. The stuccoes were done by Lorenzo Rubini (also responsible for the contemporary external decoration of the Loggia del Capitaniato) and, after his death in 1574, by his son Agostino. The overall result was a grandiose palace rivaling the residences of the Thiene, the Porto, and the Valmarana, and enabling its patron to emphasize his leading role in the Vicentine cultural élite.

In the *Historia di Vicenza* of 1591, Iacopo Marzari describes Montano Barbarano as a man 'of *belles lettres* and a most excellent musician'. In fact a 1592 inventory includes various flutes confirming that music was an important feature of life in the palace.

A comparison of the Gothic arches of the Venetian Palazzo Ducale and the loggias of Palladio's basilica (inspired by the classical language of ancient Rome) clearly reveals the Vicentine nobility's desire to underscore its cultural independence from the architectural models of *La Serenissima* (this is even more striking in the differences between the sixteenth-century palaces in Vicenza and those on the Grand Canal). Nevertheless, twenty years later, when the City Council commissioned the remodeling of the official residence of the Venetian *capitanio* (the Republic's military chief in the city), Palladio was again to be the protagonist and so the contest, in this case, was between two extraordinary pieces of architecture standing opposite each other in Piazza dei Signori. Only extremely rarely do architects have the opportunity of working twice in the same place at an interval of twenty years. The young architect of the Basilica, then still under the supervision of Giovanni da Porlezza, had now become the celebrated designer of major buildings: churches, palaces and villas for the ruling élite of the Veneto. Palladio avoided any direct dialogue between the two buildings: opposite the purity of the Basilica's two orders of arcades (built in plain white stone with only a few architectural decorative elements such as the frieze, keystones, and statues) is the Loggia's giant Composite order of half-columns restraining exuberant stucco decorations. Both the use of the giant order and this decorative richness are typical features of Palladio's language in the last decade of his life. The color contrast today between the white stone and the red brick, however (even though introduced by Palladio in the Convento della Carità, Venice), is only due to decay. In fact, extensive remains of the original light-colored stucco once covering the bricks are still quite visible just below the large Composite capitals.

Palladio's Loggia replaced a similar structure which had stood on the site since the Middle Ages and had already been reconstructed at least twice in the sixteenth century: a covered public loggia on the ground floor and an audience hall on the upper story. Funds for the new construction became available in April 1571 and work began immediately. Palladio supplied the last drawings for the molding templates in March 1572 and, by the end of the year, the building was roofed with Giannantonio Fasolo painting the lacunars in the audience hall and Lorenzo Rubini making the stuccoes and statues.

While the upper hall has a flat coffered ceiling, for the ground floor there is a complex vault covering clearly required to sustain the weight of the hall. The overall design is extremely sophisticated and includes portals which open into niches and follow their curvature.

There is little point in engaging in the sterile interminable debate over whether Palladio intended to extend the loggia to five (or seven) bays. What is altogether more interesting is Palladio's compositional freedom. He designed a radically different façade onto the Piazza compared to the front onto the Contra' del Monte, thereby undermining the building's logical unity. On closer observation, however, we see that Palladio was actually only providing effective solutions to two different situations: the piazza's broad visual frontage (also bearing in mind the constraints of the narrow elevation) inevitably suggested the powerful vertical thrust of the giant order; while the building's short sides and the smallish size of Contra' del Monte induced him to propose a smaller order for the other façade. Moreover, the Contra' del Monte façade was to be used as a kind of perennial triumphal arch marking the Venetian victory over the Turks at the battle of Lepanto in October 1571.

15.
Loggia del Capitaniato

16.
Palazzo Porto in piazza Castello

The striking part of this building forming the backdrop to Piazza del Castello is the obvious evidence of an ill-fated Palladian project. To the left of the fragment is the clearly visible old fifteenth-century house of the Porto family, which should have been gradually demolished as construction of the new palace advanced. Given the outcome, the patron Alessandro Porto's farsighted prudence is to be commended. The date is uncertain, though definitely after 1570, since the *palazzo* was not included in the *Quattro Libri* (published in Venice that year). Moreover, Alessandro only inherited the family property in Piazza Castello after the death of his father Benedetto and, at the time of the division of the family estate, with his brothers Orazio and Pompeo in 1571.

Francesco Thiene, the owner of Palladio's Palazzo Thiene at the other end of the Piazza, married Isabella Porto, Alessandro's sister. As in the cases of Iseppo Porto and his brothers-in-law Marcantonio and Adriano Thiene, the rivalry between the two families may well account for the unusual dimensions of the Palazzo Porto. Moreover, the palace's position as a backdrop to the piazza clearly required a marked monumentality in order to dominate the great open area in front. Palladio had tried out this logic a few years earlier in the Loggia del Capitaniato in Piazza dei Signori. As an analysis of the surviving walls suggests, he very likely intended to extend Palazzo Porto to seven bays and add a courtyard ending in an exedra. It is unclear why work on the palace came to a halt, but in 1615 Vincenzo Scamozzi claims he personally saw to the completion of what now survives of the building.

There are more doubts than certainties about the history of the villa Francesco Thiene built on family property at the eastern end of Strada Maggiore (today Corso Palladio), even concerning the exact date of its construction. When Palladio died the palace had still not been built: the *Pianta Angelica* of 1580 still only shows the old houses and a garden. A document of 1586 records that construction had certainly begun by 1593 and, on the death of the patron Francesco Thiene, the palace was at least a third built. Enea Thiene, who had inherited the estate of his uncle, Francesco, saw to it that the work was completed, probably within the first decade of the seventeenth century. In 1835 the palace was acquired by Lelio Bonin Longare.

In his treatise *L'idea della architettura universale* (published in Venice in 1615), Vincenzo Scamozzi writes that he was responsible for completing the building on the basis of a project by another architect (without indicating whom), but with certain unspecified revisions to the original design. The architect not named by Scamozzi is certainly Andrea Palladio, because two surviving autograph drawings clearly refer to Francesco Thiene's palace. They include two alternative plans, very close to the present building, as well as a sketch for the façade, very unlike the built front.

It is unclear when Palladio formulated his own ideas for this palace, but it was probably in 1572, the year Francesco Thiene and his uncle Orazio divided up the family property and Francesco entered into possession of the inherited site where Palladio's building would be constructed.

An analysis of the actual building reveals various elements suggesting a date in the 1570s. There are, for example, several points of contact with the Palazzo Barbaran da Porto, both in the design of the lower section of the façade and in the great two-order loggia giving onto the courtyard. According to some scholars, the side might be the work of Vincenzo Scamozzi given its affinities with the Palazzo Trissino at the cathedral. The deep atrium—substantially outside the grid of orders—could also be by Scamozzi and it is interesting to note the use of the rather irregular pre-existing walls in the rooms to the right on entering, while the rooms on the left are perfectly regular and obviously rise from new foundations.

17.
Palazzo Thiene-Bonin Longare

18.
Valmarana Chapel

Palladio probably designed this delicate chapel following Antonio Valmarana's death in 1576. It is situated in the crypt of the church of Santa Corona, which had been the traditional burial place for the Valmarana family for fifty years. Ten years earlier Palladio had been responsible for building the great family palace (on what is now Corso Fogazzaro) for Antonio's parents and, by 1574, Antonio himself was certainly living there. The date 1597 inscribed on a paving stone does not, therefore, refer to the date of construction, but rather to when Leonardo Valmarana moved the remains of his parents and brothers to the chapel. In fact, Leonardo mentions in his will that he had been responsible for its construction. Although there is no direct documentary attribution, the Cappella Valmarana is undoubtedly by Palladio. Its carefully balanced space is almost like a miniature hypogeum. Bounded by book-folded pilasters with double entasis, the square chamber extends longitudinally with two niches surmounted by embrasures filtering a sepulchral light—a sophisticated citation of the *tablinum* found in antique Roman houses. Around the same time, Palladio designed the side chapels for the church of the Redentore in Venice with a sequence of spaces very similar to those in the Cappella Valmarana, suggesting that the Vicenza chapel might almost have been a kind of prototype.

19.
Arco delle Scalette

The genesis and even the name of the architect of this arch are far from clear. Before the mid-eighteenth century construction of the porticoes by Francesco Muttoni, the arch marked the beginning of the path to the sanctuary of Monte Berico. What does appear to be certain is the date of construction (1595) and the patron, the Venetian captain, Giacomo Bragadino. Equally well documented are the requests made by the friars of the sanctuary from 1574 to 1576 for financial support from the community in order to reconstruct the entire stepped path (the so-called *scalette*) to Monte Berico. There is no evidence, however, that the arch was actually included in the general reconstruction that also included the sanctuary itself. Nor is the original form of the arch known. Seventeenth-century images show it with frontal niches, later moved to the intrados to make room for the *Annunciation* by Orazio Marinali.

In 1578 the Vicentine noble Lodovico Trento earmarked a sizable sum of money for the reconstruction of a small church attached to the Augustinian convent of Santa Maria Nova in Borgo Porta Nuova, to the west of the city. By 1590, twelve years later, the church had been completed and was decorated with canvases by foremost artists like Maffei, the Maganzas, Andrea Vicentino, and Carpioni. Under construction from 1539, the convent was a leading institution of its kind in the city and offered hospitality to many daughters from noble Vicentine families, such as the Valmarana, Piovene, Angarano, Revese, Garzadori, and Monza.

Although there are no surviving documents or autograph drawings proving Palladio designed the church, the building was very likely based on a project he drafted around 1578, which was built (after his death in 1580) under the supervision of the master mason Domenico Groppino whose name appears in the relevant documentation. Furthermore, in 1583, Montano Barbarano—the patron of the palace by Palladio in the Contra' Porti—also contributed a large sum for the construction of the church of the convent (which accommodated his two daughters) and Domenico Groppino is known to have been Montano's tried and trusted mason.

The evidence of the architecture itself excludes the possibility that a simple *capomastro* like Groppino could have been the architect. The church has a single nave, in the form of an ancient temple cella, entirely bounded by Corinthian half-columns on plinths. It closely resembles the Roman temple at Nîmes which Palladio had drawn in the *Quattro Libri*. The power and inventive freedom of the interior and façade clearly suggest the hand of Palladio. A straightforward imitation would have used a much more conventional register. On the other hand, a number of errors and weaknesses in the construction should probably be ascribed to Groppino.

20.
Church of Santa Maria Nova

21.
Teatro Olimpico

Founded in 1556, the Accademia Olimpica would have to wait over twenty years before constructing its permanent theater to put on performances previously staged on temporary wooden structures in palace courtyards or in the *salone* of the Palazzo della Ragione. Only in 1580, in fact, did the Accademia begin work on the theater (on land near the Isola ceded by the City Council) designed by their own academician, Andrea Palladio. In August of that year, however, the architect died and was never to see the finished building, which was completed by his son Silla.

After Palladio, Vincenzo Scamozzi also worked on the theater, inserting beyond the proscenium the sets (prepared for the inaugural performance of *The Seven Roads of Thebes* in 1585) which thereafter remained an integral part of the building. Recent studies have demonstrated that Palladio's original design made provisions only for a single perspective in line with the central portal of the proscenium, while painted backdrops were intended to fill the two side openings. The apertures in the two side walls and the lacunar ceiling above the stage also date from Palladio's project.

The Teatro Olimpico was the realization of a dream pursued by generations of Renaissance humanists and architects to give permanent form to one of the great symbolic building types in the classical cultural tradition. Palladio's design reconstructed the typical Roman theater with an archaeological accuracy acquired by thoroughly studying Vitruvius and the ruins of ancient theatrical complexes. In this sense, it is a kind of spiritual legacy of the great Vicentine architect. The Teatro Olimpico brings back to life the theater of the ancients. In this work Palladio achieves an absolute affinity with the language of great classical architecture. It is the outcome of a life spent seeking—through "long labors, great industry and love"—the laws of that language's secret harmony.

Info

1.
Villa Trissino at Cricoli
strada Marosticana 6,
Vicenza
Tel. +39 0444 323014
Public not admitted.
Groups and scholars
admitted on demand,
to CISA or to other public
or official institutions

2.
**Church of Santa Maria
dei Servi**
via Roma, Padova
Tel. +39 049 8750781
Visits: working days
7.45-12 am / 4-7.15 pm
Sundays and Bank Holidays
9-12.30 am / 2-7 pm
For guided tours please
contact the Volunteers
service at +39 348 3904203

3.
Palazzo Civena
viale Eretenio 12, Vicenza
Outside visits only

4.
Palazzo Pojana
corso Palladio 92-96, Vicenza
Outside visits only

5.
Palazzo Thiene
contra' S. Gaetano Thiene 11,
Vicenza
Tel. +39 0444 542131
Fax +39 0444 544519
toll-free calls 800 297886
www.palazzothiene.it
palazzothiene@popvi.it
Visits: October to April
Tuesdays and Wednesdays
9-12 am / 3-6 pm
May to September
Wednesdays and Fridays
9-12 am / 3-6 pm
Saturdays 9-12 am
Closed in July and August
and on any weekday coinciding
with a Bank Holiday

Groups (max 20 people)
and guided visits by
appointment only

6.
Palazzo Iseppo Porto
contra' Porti 21, Vicenza
Outside visits only

7.
Palazzo della Ragione
piazza dei Signori, Vicenza
Outside visits only

8.
Palazzo Chiericati
piazza Matteotti 37-39,
Vicenza
Tel. +39 0444 325071
Visits: July to August
Tuesday to Sunday
9 am – 6 pm
September to June
Tuesday to Sunday
9 am – 5 pm

9.
Vicenza Cathedral
piazza Duomo, Vicenza
Tel. +39 0444 325007 (sacristy)
Visits: every day
9-12 am / 3.30-7 pm
Sundays and Bank Holidays
3.30-5.15 pm / 6-7.15 pm
Visit are not allowed during
worship

10.
Palazzo Schio
contra' San Marco 39,
Vicenza
Outside visits only

11.
**Casa Cogollo, or
'Palladio's House'**
corso Palladio 165-167,
Vicenza
Outside visits only

12.
Palazzo Valmarana
corso Fogazzaro 16,
Vicenza
Tel. +39 0444 547188 (am only)
Fax +39 0444 23172
Mob. +39 347 7204658
www.palazzovalmaranabraga.it
Visits: Wednesdays
10–12 am / 3-6 pm
Groups (min 15 people) by
appointment only

13.
**Villa Almerico Capra,
or 'La Rotonda'**
via della Rotonda 45, Vicenza
Tel. +39 0444 321793 /
+39 049 8790879
Fax +39 049 8791380
Visits:
15th March to 4th November
Tuesday to Sunday
10-12 am / 3-6 pm
on Wednesdays also interior
Visits at different times
may be arranged by
appointment (at least 4
weeks in advance)

14.
Palazzo Barbaran
contra' Porti 11, Vicenza
Tel. +39 0444 323014
Fax +39 0444 322869
www.cisapalladio.org
Visits: 1st November to
Easter, Tuesday to Thursday
10 am – 4 pm
Friday to Sunday
10 am – 5 pm
From Easter to 20th September
Wednesday to Sunday
10 am – 6 pm
Closed on Mondays

15.
Loggia del Capitaniato
piazza dei Signori, Vicenza
Outside visits only

16.
**Palazzo Porto in piazza
Castello**
piazza Castello 18, Vicenza
Outside visits only

17.
**Palazzo Thiene-Bonin
Longare**
corso Palladio 13, Vicenza
Outside visits only

18.
Valmarana Chapel
Church di Santa Corona,
contra' Santa Corona,
Vicenza
Visits: From Monday to
Sunday, 8.30-12 am / 2.30-
6.30 pm. Visit are not
allowed during worship

19.
Arco delle Scalette
piazzale Fraccon, Vicenza

20.
**Church of Santa Maria
Nova**
contrada Santa Maria
Nova, Vicenza

21.
Teatro Olimpico
piazza Matteotti, Vicenza
Tel. +39 0444 222800
Visits: July to August
Tuesday to Sunday
9 am – 6 pm
September to June
Tuesday to Sunday
10 am – 5 pm

Bibliography

Giangiorgio Zorzi,
*I disegni delle antichità
di Andrea Palladio*, Vicenza
1959.

Giangiorgio Zorzi,
*Le opere pubbliche
e i palazzi privati di Andrea
Palladio*, Venice 1965.

James Ackerman, *Palladio*,
Harmondsworth 1966.

Giangiorgio Zorzi,
*Le chiese e i ponti
di Andrea Palladio*, Vicenza
1966.

Giangiorgio Zorzi,
*Le ville e i teatri di Andrea
Palladio*, Venice 1969.

Lionello Puppi, *Andrea
Palladio. L'opera completa*,
Milan 1973.

Howard Burns
(edited by), *Andrea Palladio
1508-1580. The Portico
and the Farmyard*, exh.
cat., in collaboration with
Lynda Fairbairn and Bruce
Boucher, London 1975.

Bruce Boucher,
*Andrea Palladio.
The Architect in his time*,
New York 1994.

Guido Beltramini, Howard
Burns, Marco Gaiani
(edited by), *Andrea
Palladio. Le ville*, cd-rom,
Vicenza 1997.

Donata Battilotti,
*Aggiornamento del
catalogo delle opere*, in
Lionello Puppi, *Andrea
Palladio. L'opera completa*,
Milan 1999.

Guido Beltramini, Antonio
Padoan (edited by), *Andrea
Palladio. Atlante delle
architetture*, Venice 2000.

Donata Battilotti, *Le chiese
di Palladio. La terraferma
veneta e l'opera di Palladio*,
in Claudia Conforti, Richard
J. Tuttle (edited by), *Storia
dell'Architettura italiana. Il
secondo Cinquecento*,
Milan 2001.

Howard Burns, *"Da
naturale inclinatione
guidato": il primo decennio
di attività di Palladio
architetto*, in Arnaldo
Bruschi (edited by), *Storia
dell'arte italiana. Il primo
Cinquecento*, Milan 2002.

Donata Battilotti, Guido
Beltramini, Howard Burns,
Marco Gaiani (edited by),
Palladio e Vicenza, cd-rom,
Vicenza 2002.

Franco Barbieri,
*Architetture palladiane.
Dalla grafica del cantiere
alle immagini del trattato*,
Vicenza 1992.

Howard Burns, *Palladio e
la villa*, in Guido
Beltramini, Howard Burns
(edited by), *Andrea Palladio
e la villa veneta da
Petrarca a Carlo Scarpa*,
exh. cat., Venice 2005.

Tracy Cooper, *Palladio's
Venice*, New Haven-London
2005.

Guido Beltramini, *Palladio
privato*, Venice 2008.

Guido Beltramini, Howard
Burns (edited by), *Palladio*,
Venice 2008.

Photolitography
Fotolito Veneta, San Martino Buonalbergo (Verona)

Printed by
La Grafica & Stampa editrice s.r.l., Vicenza
for Marsilio Editori® s.p.a. in Venezia

EDITION

10 9 8 7 6 5 4 3 2

YEAR

2008   2009   2010   2011